Fun with Clothes

Ropas divertidas

Vêtements au plaisir

夏天的衣服，遊戲的衣服

text by Ruth Fahlman
photos by May Henderson and Ruth Fahlman

Addison Wesley

Toronto

What are you going to wear today?

Qu'est-ce que tu vas porter aujourd'hui?

¿Qué ropa vas a ponerte hoy?

你今天要穿什麼衣服？

Clothes that you wear underneath all the rest?

Les vêtements que tu portes en dessous de tous les autres?

¿Ropa interior que usas debajo de otras prendas?

你會穿什麼內衣褲？

Clothes that you wear when you go out to play?

Les vêtements que tu portes lorsque tu joues dehors?

¿Ropas que usas cuando vas a jugar afuera?

你穿什麼衣服出去遊戲？

Clothes that you wear when you want to pretend?

Les vêtements que tu portes lorsque tu te déguises?

¿Ropas que usas cuando quieres disfrazarte?

你穿什麼衣服去化裝？

Clothes that you wear when you want to stay warm?

Les vêtements que tu portes lorsqu'il fait froid?

¿Ropas que usas cuando quieres abrigarte?

你穿什麼衣服可以保暖？

Clothes that you wear when you're going to get wet?

Les vêtements que tu portes lorsque tu te baignes?

¿Ropas que usas cuando vas a mojarte?

在你將會濕身時，你會穿什麼衣服？

Clothes that you wear in traditional ways?

Les vêtements que tu portes de façon traditionnelle?

¿Ropas que usas tradicionalmente?

你穿什麼傳統的衣服？

Clothes that you wear for parties or visits?

Les vêtements que tu portes lorsque tu fais la fête?

¿Ropas que usas para fiestas o visitas?

你穿什麼衣服去宴會或作客？

Clothes that you wear in a play or a dance?

Les vêtements que tu portes lorsque tu fais du théâtre ou de la danse?

¿Ropas que usas en una obra de teatro o en un baile?

你穿什麼衣服去表演或跳舞？

Clothes that you wear when you're ready for bed?

Les vêtements que tu portes lorsque tu te couches?

¿Ropas que usas cuando estas listo para ir a la cama?

你穿什麼衣服去睡覺？

So many choices! What are you wearing today?

Que de choix! Qu'est-ce que tu portes aujourd'hui?

¡Tantas alternativas! ¿Qué estás usando hoy?

那麼多選擇！你今天穿什麼？

Sponsoring Editor: Beth Bruder

Designer: Pamela Kinney

Editor: Lauren E. Wolk

Translators

Spanish: Edith Stagni
           Brenda Cortes

French: Katherine Stauble
         Martine Brassard

Chinese: Mei-lin Cheung
          Sew Pim Lim
          Hsiao Chiang

Sponsor: Early Childhood Multicultural Services

Early Childhood Multicultural Services gratefully acknowledges the support and financial assistance of the Multiculturalism Directorate, Secretary of State, Canada; the Cabinet Committee on Cultural Heritage, Province of British Columbia; and the Preschool ESL Committee (PRESL), Vancouver.

Canadian Cataloguing in Publication Data

Fahlman, Ruth, 1954–
    Fun with clothes

(Hand in hand)
Text in English, Chinese, French, Spanish.
ISBN 0-201-54650-7 (set). – ISBN 0-201-54660-4 (School Edition)
ISBN 0-201-54744-9 (Trade Edition)

1. Clothing and dress – Juvenile literature.
I. Henderson, May. II. Title. III. Series:
Hand in hand (Don Mills, Ont.).

GT518.F34 1990   391   C90-094221-5

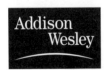
ISBN 0-201-54660-4

Printed in Canada

1 2 3 4 5 G   06 05 04 03 02